ALTERNATOR BOOKS™

DIGITAL SAFETY SMARTS

USING SOCIAL MEDIA

Dan Kingsley

Lerner Publications ◆ Minneapolis

Lerner Publications Company
An imprint of Lerner Publishing Group, Inc.
241 First Avenue North
Minneapolis, MN 55401 USA

For reading levels and more information, look up this title at www.lernerbooks.com.

Main body text set in Aptifer Sans LT Pro
Typeface provided by Linotype.

Library of Congress Cataloging-in-Publication Data

Names: Kingsley, Dan, author.
Title: Using social media / Dan Kingsley.
Description: Minneapolis, MN : Lerner Publications, 2025. | Series: Digital safety smarts (alternator books) | Includes bibliographical references and index. | Audience term: Preteens | Audience term: School children | Audience: Ages 8–12 | Audience: Grades 4–6 | Summary: "Social media is fun and exciting, but it also has plenty of downsides. Readers will learn about their digital footprint, the importance of keeping their personal information private, and much more"—Provided by publisher.
Identifiers: LCCN 2024043992 (print) | LCCN 2024043993 (ebook) | ISBN 9798765668276 (library binding) | ISBN 9798765683880 (paperback) | ISBN 9798765676493 (epub)
Subjects: LCSH: Social media and youth—Juvenile literature.
Classification: LCC HQ799.2.S59 K56 2025 (print) | LCC HQ799.2.S59 (ebook) | DDC 302.23/10835—dc23/eng/20250130

LC record available at https://lccn.loc.gov/2024043992
LC ebook record available at https://lccn.loc.gov/2024043993

Manufactured in the United States of America
1 – CG – 7/15/25

TABLE OF CONTENTS

INTRODUCTION

YOU CAN'T TAKE IT BACK

Mia stared at her phone screen, her heart racing. She had just received a text from her friend, Caden.

"I failed the math test. I don't know what happened."

Mia felt bad for Caden, but she also thought it might make others feel better to know even the "smart kids" struggle sometimes. Without thinking, she posted it on social media.

"Guess who failed their math test? Even the class genius has off days!"

Within minutes, comments started pouring in.

"No way! Caden failed?"

"Not so smart I guess!"

"Maybe he should spend less time playing video games!"

Posting a message on social media that you wish you could take back can make you feel awful.

Mia's excitement at the attention her post was getting quickly turned sour when she received another text, this one from Caden.

"Mia! Why did you share that? Now everyone knows, and my parents saw it too."

Mia's stomach churned. She hadn't meant to hurt Caden or get him in trouble. She realized too late that she'd shared something personal and private without permission.

As Mia frantically tried to delete the post, more comments came in, some supportive but others not. Mia felt terrible, but the damage was already done.

Have you ever been in Mia's or Caden's position?

Social media can be exciting, but also tricky! This book will explore using social media safely, kindly, and smartly. You'll learn to protect your privacy, share positively, and handle online problems.

Let's get started!

How old were you when you got your first social media account? On average, kids are about twelve and a half when they get one.

CHAPTER ONE

UNDERSTANDING SOCIAL MEDIA

Social media is an unlimited online playground. You can chat with friends, discover and share content, learn about cool things from all over the world, and more. It's a collection of websites and apps that lets people interact, create, and share things they love online.

Many social media platforms require you to be thirteen years or older, or require the permission of a parent, to create an account. These social platforms are like virtual hangout spots where you can post anything you want, from updates about your day to how good your new sneakers look. You can comment on your friends' posts. You can also join groups that you like and play games with others.

Unlike watching TV or reading a book where you're just taking in information, with social media you can choose to

GLOBAL APPEAL

Over five billion people use social media worldwide! On average, users spend more than two hours a day checking their accounts.

interact with others. There are four main types of social media platforms.

- Social networks: The most common type of social media platform, these let you create a personal profile, connect with friends, and share all sorts of content. For example, Facebook and Instagram are well-known social networks.
- Messaging apps: These focus on private chats between individuals or small groups. WhatsApp and Snapchat are popular choices.
- Video sharing platforms: They involve watching and sharing videos. YouTube and TikTok are big examples.
- Gaming platforms: These combine playing games with social features like being able to chat and have friends lists. *Roblox* and *Minecraft* are huge with gamers.

Making TikTok videos is a popular activity for many young people.

Why We Use Social Media

People love social media because it helps them stay in touch with friends and family wherever they are in the world. You can chat with your best friend even when you're not at school, see photos of your cousin's new puppy, and send a funny meme to make your sibling laugh.

You can join a group about your favorite book series, watch tutorials on how to draw your favorite cartoon characters, or even share photos of a cool creation you just built.

Social media gives you the opportunity to let the people in your life know how you're doing in fun and creative ways.

The Two Sides of Social Media

When used responsibly, social media can be super fun and even educational. You can learn new things from people all over the world, express your unique creativity, and stay up to date on news and trends. You can also stay connected and meet more people online.

Social media can also have downsides. This includes online predators, cyberbullying, sharing too much personal information, or spending too much time online and ignoring other important things.

The internet is a place where people can be mean or cruel, including on social media.

CHAPTER TWO

PRIVACY AND YOUR DIGITAL FOOTPRINT

Private information is stuff about you that shouldn't be shared with everyone. It's like a secret you only tell your closest friends or family. Certain things are kept private for safety reasons.

Your private information includes:

- Full name and address
- Phone number
- Passwords
- School name and location
- Family details

Why keep it private? That's because bad people might use this information to trick you, harm you, or cause trouble.

To protect your privacy, use strong passwords (a mix of letters, numbers, and symbols), and set your accounts to

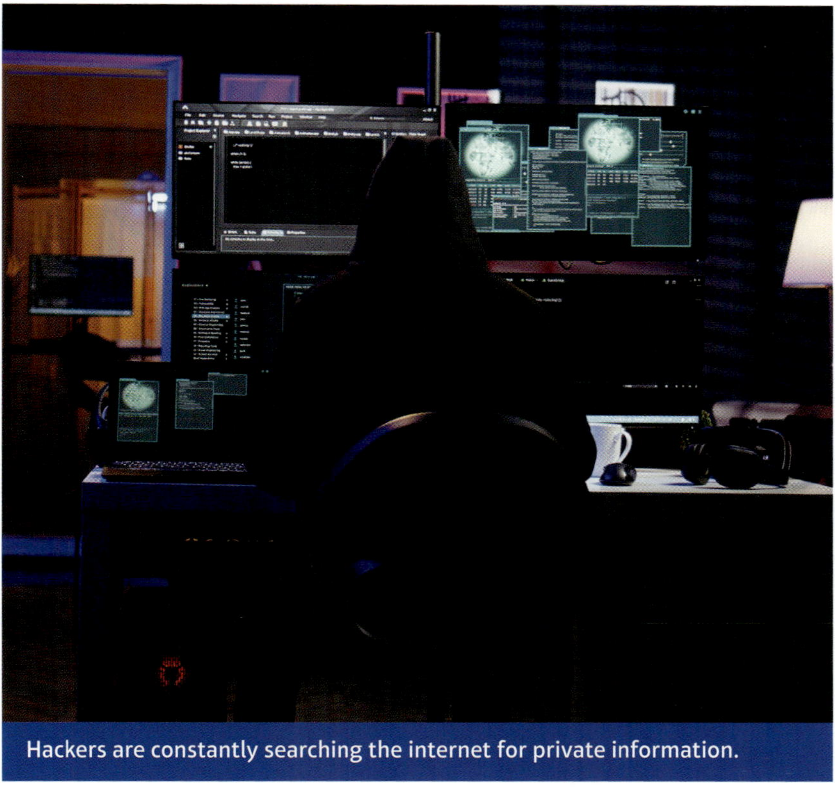

Hackers are constantly searching the internet for private information.

"private" so only friends can see what you post. Never share passwords, even with friends, and ask a parent before sharing any personal information online.

Even innocent-seeming posts can give away too much. A photo of you in your school uniform or outside your house could tell strangers where to find you.

DID YOU KNOW?

Two-factor authentication adds extra security by requiring two separate identifiers, like a password plus a code sent to your phone or email, for account access.

WHAT NOT TO SHARE ONLINE

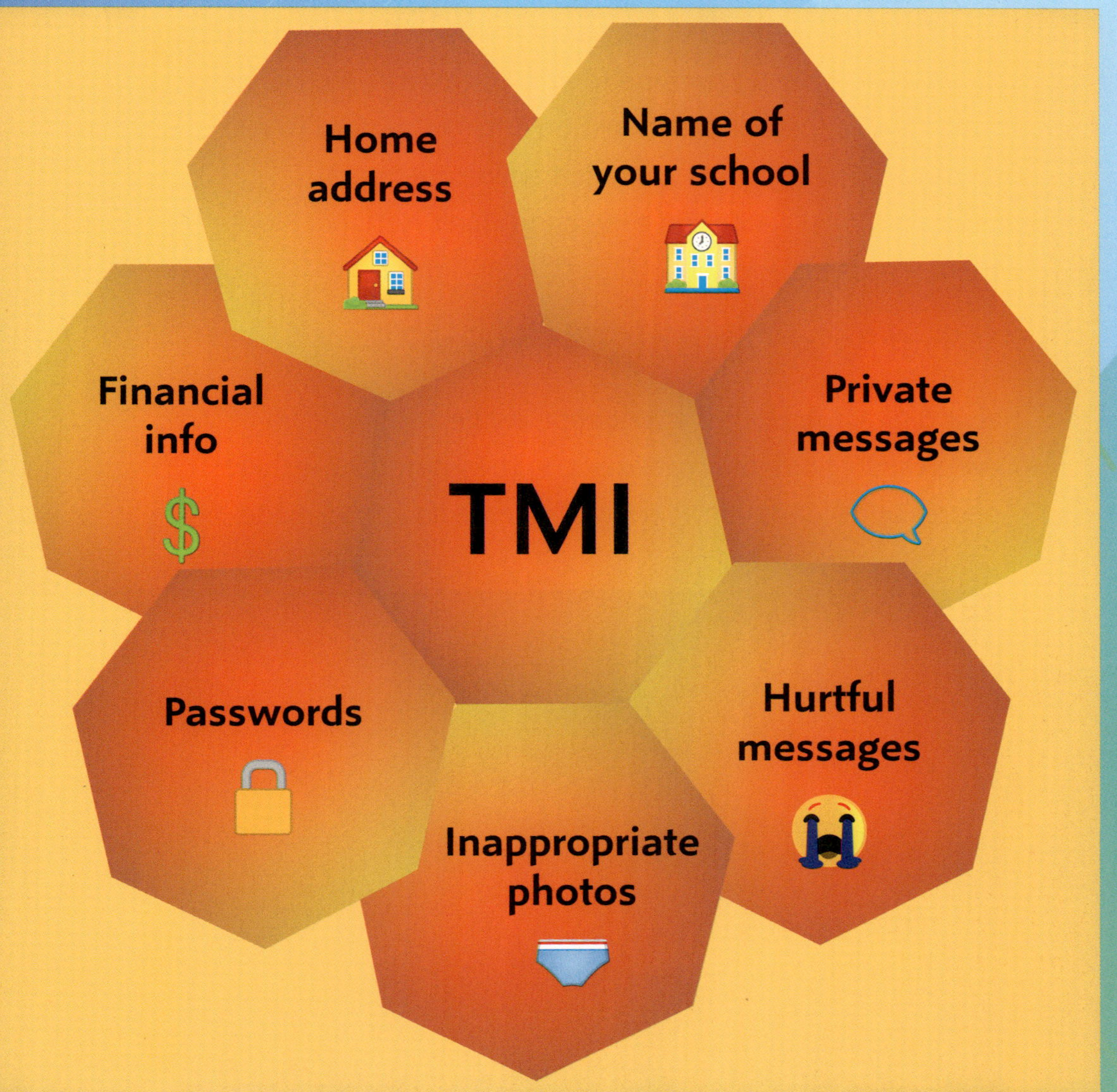

Avoid oversharing! Keep this stuff private.

Stranger Danger

Just like in the real world, it's also not safe to talk to strangers online. Some people pretend to be kids to trick you. They might ask for personal information or try to get you to meet in person. These people are called online predators.

If a stranger sends you a message, don't respond. Block them if possible and tell a trusted adult right away.

What Is a Digital Footprint?

Your digital footprint is your online image. It is made up of everything about you that exists on the internet. It includes photos and videos you've posted, comments you've made,

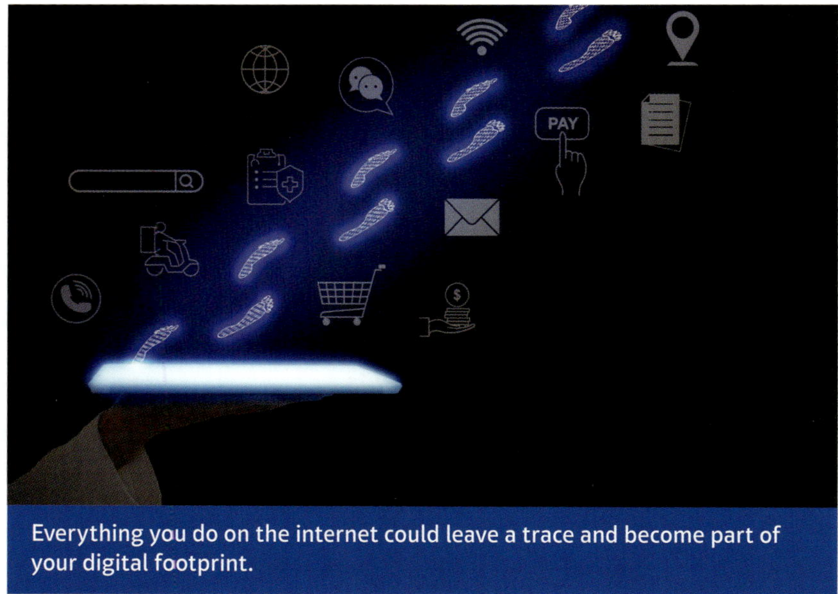

Everything you do on the internet could leave a trace and become part of your digital footprint.

and posts that you have been tagged in.

Your digital footprint can last forever! Future teachers, coaches, college administrators, or even employers might form opinions about you based on your digital footprint. That's why it's important to keep it positive.

An example of a good post would be sharing a photo of your science fair project. A bad example would be sharing an embarrassing picture of a friend without their permission.

Pictures about your hobbies or accomplishments are perfect subjects for a social media post.

CHAPTER THREE

HOW YOUR ONLINE ACTIVITY AFFECTS YOUR FUTURE

There are many things to consider when you've got your finger hovering over that "post" button. How will it affect the people in the post? How might it affect you?

Think of your social media posts like snapshots in time. Even if one is deleted, someone could have already saved or shared that snapshot. That's why it's important to think about how your posts might affect you or others in the future. The mindset you should have is that social media is permanent. So, always ask yourself: "Would I be okay with everyone seeing this forever?"

Don't let former posts come back to haunt you. College admissions agents and even future employers might check your social media and deny you because of bad posts, so don't put anything out there you might regret.

IN THE SPOTLIGHT

The Regretful Post

Paula, age 14, loved posting funny memes. One day, she created a meme that was a mean joke about her math teacher. She thought it was harmless, but the post went viral.

Two years later, Paula applied for a summer job at a math tutoring center. The owner searched Paula's name online and found the popular old post. Even though Paula had grown since then and was excellent at math, the owner worried about hiring someone who behaved like this online.

Paula didn't get the job.

Digital Citizenship

Being a good digital citizen means using the internet in a kind and responsible way. You can share positive and uplifting content, compliment others, and encourage friends. Don't be afraid to stand up against bullying and share helpful information or resources where needed.

The best way to respect people's privacy and boundaries is to always ask before posting information about them. Don't share screenshots of private conversations. Always ask permission before posting content about someone. Be sure to respect it when someone asks you to remove a post about them. Also, don't pressure others to share things they're uncomfortable with.

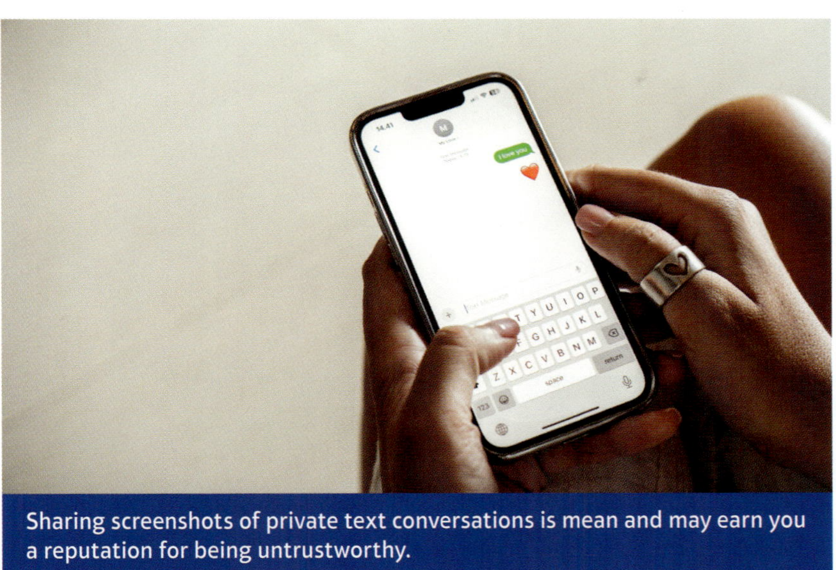

Sharing screenshots of private text conversations is mean and may earn you a reputation for being untrustworthy.

Creating a Positive Online Presence

Your online presence is like your digital personality. Here are some ways to make it shine:

- Sharing a photo of a volunteer activity you participated in
- Posting about a book, movie, or video you enjoyed and why you recommend it
- Creating a fun, family-friendly video challenge
- Sharing tips or tutorials related to a hobby (like art or coding)
- Posting about a goal you achieved

Remember, your online presence reflects who you are to the outside world.

A pic of yourself having fun with your friends would make a good social media post. But ask them if it's OK to post first!

The Negative Side

Social media is a relatively new technology, so its long-term effects are still unclear. However, there are some studies that show a strong link between heavy social media use and increased risk of depression, anxiety, loneliness, self-harm, and suicidal thoughts.

Social media can create negative feelings such as being unhappy about your life or appearance. These feelings can be caused by comparing your life to what you see online. But many images others post are edited, made using artificial intelligence, or only show the best moments of someone's life. So it's important to remember that social media does not show the whole story. People can pretend to have "perfect" lives online, but this is not the case in real life.

Try to focus on keeping your own online presence positive and real rather than comparing it with others. Spending less time online and more time with real-life friends can help.

Between Photoshop, filters, and AI, you never know how real images in social media posts are.

CHAPTER FOUR

ACTIONS MATTER

Just like in real life, it's important to be considerate of others online. When you tag someone in a post or share something about them, pause to think about how they might feel. Consider if it might embarrass them, and always ask yourself if they'd want everyone else to see it.

Kindness and Bullying Online

Words can hurt, even when they're just on a screen. In fact, they might hurt even more because online messages can be seen by lots of people. They can also be saved and shared, lasting longer than spoken words.

If someone is being mean to you online, don't respond or try to get revenge. Save evidence of the bullying, such as screenshots, then block the person if possible and tell a trusted adult right away.

Posting hurtful words on social media is cyberbullying, and it can have serious consequences.

Helping Friends Stay Safe

Compliment and encourage your friends' positive posts, speak up if you see someone being unkind to others, and remind friends to be careful about what they share if you notice oversharing.

If you see something that seems wrong or dangerous, use the app's Report function if available. Tell a trusted adult about what you saw and encourage your friends to report harmful content too, because we stay safer when we look out for each other.

Always remember - the internet is forever. Think before you post.

SOCIAL MEDIA SAFETY CHECKLIST

DO
set your profiles to private

DON'T
share personal information such as your phone number or address

DO
only add people you know personally

DON'T
post inappropriate content

DO
report concerning behavior to a trusted adult right away

DON'T
arrange in-person meetups with people you only know online

DO
think before you post

DON'T
engage with or respond to bullies or strangers

Now you know how to connect with friends, express yourself creatively, and have tons of fun on social media while staying safe and treating other people with respect.

Remember before you post anything, always T.H.I.N.K.: is it **T**rue? **H**elpful? **I**nspiring? **N**ecessary? or **K**ind?

THINKing first will help you make using social media a fun and safe activity.

Capturing the moment! 📸 Remember, social media is about fun and connection, so always share with respect and kindness to keep it safe for everyone.

When used properly, social media can be an entertaining way to keep in touch with friends.

GLOSSARY

cyberbullying: the use of electronic communication to bully, or to be mean to someone

digital citizen: a person who uses the internet regularly, kindly, and safely

digital footprint: all the stuff you create about yourself while using the internet

meme: a funny image, video, or text that is copied and shared by lots of people online

oversharing: giving away too much personal information about yourself or someone else, especially online

privacy settings: ways to control who can see your posts within social media platforms

profile: your online personal page on a social media platform where people learn about you or where you learn about other people

social media: online platforms, or websites and apps where you can talk to friends and share things

tag: mentioning someone in a social media post, often linking to their profile and telling them of the content

viral: a post that spreads quickly across the internet, typically through social media sharing

LEARN MORE

Bathie, Holly. *Social Media Survival Guide*. London: Usborne, 2024.

BrainPop
https://www.brainpop.com/technology/digitalcitizenship/digitaletiquette/

Clark, Katie. *Dealing With Online Bullies*. Minneapolis: Lerner Publishing, 2026.

Debbink, Andrea. *Think for Yourself: The Ultimate Guide to Critical Thinking in an Age of Information Overload and Misinformation*. Baltimore: duopress, 2020.

KidsHealth
https://kidshealth.org/en/kids/

NetSmartz Kids
https://www.netsmartzkids.org

Pearlman, Catherine. *First Phone: A Child's Guide to Digital Responsibility, Safety, and Etiquette*. New York: TarcherPerigee, 2022.

Protect Us Kids
https://www.pukyouthlife.org/

INDEX

PHOTO ACKNOWLEDGMENTS

Image credits: fizkes/Shutterstock, p. 5; fizkes/Shutterstock, p. 6; Inside Creative House/Shutterstock, p. 8; Nattakorn_Maneerat/Shutterstock, p. 9; Kaspars Grinvalds/Shutterstock, p. 10; Antonio Guillem/Shutterstock, p. 11; DC Studio/Shutterstock, p. 13; Shutter z/Shutterstock, p. 14; Ole.CNX/Shutterstock, p.16; Hero Images Inc/Shutterstock, p. 17; KinoMasterskaya/Shutterstock, p. 19; moonmovie/Shutterstock, p. 21; PeopleImages.com - Yuri A/Shutterstcok, p. 22; MDV Edwards/Shutterstock, p. 23; Prostock-studio/Shutterstock, p. 25; stoatphoto/Shutterstock, p. 26; Drazen Zigic/Shutterstock, p. 28; Ground Picture/Shutterstock, p. 29; Just dance/Shutterstock, p. 31. Cover image: Dragon Images/Shutterstock.